About the Author

A tenacious wordsmith who, amidst the complexities of mental health, embarked on a poetic journey, drawing inspiration from the enchanting wonders of nature and the ethereal realm of romanticism.

Mahler's Cigarettes

Benjamin Szijártó

Mahler's Cigarettes

Olympia Publishers
London

www.olympiapublishers.com
OLYMPIA PAPERBACK EDITION

Copyright © Benjamin Szijártó 2024

The right of Benjamin Szijártó to be identified as author of
this work has been asserted in accordance with sections 77 and 78 of
the Copyright, Designs and Patents Act 1988.

All Rights Reserved

No reproduction, copy or transmission of this publication
may be made without written permission.
No paragraph of this publication may be reproduced,
copied or transmitted save with the written permission of the publisher,
or in accordance with the provisions
of the Copyright Act 1956 (as amended).

Any person who commits any unauthorised act in relation to
this publication may be liable to criminal
prosecution and civil claims for damage.

A CIP catalogue record for this title is
available from the British Library.

ISBN: 978-1-80439-714-5

This is a work of fiction.
Names, characters, places and incidents originate from the writer's
imagination. Any resemblance to actual persons, living or dead, is
purely coincidental.

First Published in 2024

**Olympia Publishers
Tallis House
2 Tallis Street
London
EC4Y 0AB**

Printed in Great Britain

Dedication

This book is dedicated to Andrew, a soul that made my heart flutter in many ways.

Acknowledgements

I'd like to thank the Romantics, for showing me a world full of love, and teaching me to find pride in pain, that you can, and will overcome. Thank you to Andrew, for encouraging me to keep writing, and inspiring me with late night chats, that made me realize how beautifully love can hurt.

A

Another day and another
Night
December's coming, isn't that
Right?
Everlasting love is due
With you, with only you

Don't let go now, swallow me
with you is where I want to be
take my hand dear, kiss me soft
of your eyes I think so oft

Be my anchor is life's a sea
trembling lips and shaking knee
breath so warm you make me shiver
your tongue, my neck, endless river

Shine so bright in autumn sky
by your side my best I try
hold me close and place a kiss
on my pillow that will miss
smiles we shared and endless nights

Marlboro

Burning cigarette in my hand
in front of us, endless land
my robe fits you like
the stars fit the night sky

Your lips taste like cherry
this moment is saint and merry
shaking in November
your smile is remedy

The kitchen is cozy and warm
you can do no harm
we sing along to love songs
as if we are not falling

Under blankets we hide
my cold hands you guide
feels like I was meant to be
next to you through the night

Tired kiss we share
alone it is hard to bare
warm bodies pressed together
I fall asleep to dream of you

Chianti

You fill my lungs with sunshine
strawberry scented spilled wine
I dry it up as I would do right
with my tears late at night

Closed eyes, I still see your face
endless beauty, you're pure grace
sharp is the cold night, hold me now
to love Oh, I don't know how
My love is poison, toxic dust
heart covered in ancient rust

November 28th

Is it just temporary bliss
how you offered me a kiss
warm and eager lips
oh how much I miss

The one who held me late at night
but alone I am and that's all right
chest pounding, hearts are aching
autumn skies are slowly fading

Cold are your hands, breath is freezing
eyes of ocean, my body teasing
it's cold and frosty, you will leave me

Evanescence

Thine voice, remedy for shattered soul
in neverending throes
yelling harrowing demons, broken prayers
of my woes
My sanity forsake me, I ache for
anchor on this sea
Heart throbbing for the slightest
of life-giving glee

Solemnize the stars, bursting into flames
drowsy rain obliterate my lethal-childish blames
Tie a know from dandelion, scented tender air
lastly hold these wounded hands they, forever care

And years later when I
mourned your loss ready
I will give my best to try
not to breathe so heavy

Simultaneous

Never stop talking
melody to my ear
with gentle hands you
wipe away my tears

Soft embrace I fall
in arms made of heaven
closer to you I crawl
the clock is ticking seven

Gaze in ocean eyes
whisper little secrets
hear my silent cries
demolish the regrets

Place your lips on mine
fierce as summer creek
quiver down my spine
I reach the highest peak

Ocean

How is there no fish in your eyes
frenzied ocean I see
no wonder we share smiles
my chest is filled with glee

Placid waters with stars
shining in your skull
reconcile the wounded hearts
the night is turning pale and dull

The sky shimmers back at me
interlock our gaze
hold me close and let me be
lost in foggy maze

You Left

You left yourself in the sheets
and rainy busy streets
I can still taste you in my mug
you left without a hug

You are soft air
between two cigarettes
I think there's still hair
on my pillow that doesn't forget

In the kitchen I see you
or the Christmas light that's new
red yellow blue and green
as you would have said "keen"

Your coat still has a place
or on my couch your space
that's way too big for me
you in the morning sky I see

Slippers that I'll never wear
this loneliness is hard to bear
I see you in every shirt
my shoes covered in dirt

I asked him, "Do you love me still?"
"You want me to?" he replied.
Oh my flower, may I bury my face in thine chest tonight?
I asked him, "Would you long after me?"
He whispered, "I would."
It was as easy and silly in the autumn as it should
In frosty hands I held his delicate ones,
murmured to ocean eyes I'm seeing
"Without you I'm not alive, just barely breathing."

Staring at the moon
silver mist the sky

Staring at the ceiling
dripping sunshine

Holding your memory
clinging to the dream

Cold is the night
my heart still melts

Empty is my bed
I'm missing you crazy

No clouds in the sky
and my vision's hazy

You are all the words
post it note on wall

Without you here
in this night I fall

Your lack of presence tastes like
dark chocolate and berries
or that beer with cherries

Silence is Mahler's 9th
my heart slowly breaks
that is all it takes

Heavenly ocean eyes
in them I'm still lost
the colour I love the most

I missed my train but it
wasn't as bad as missing
you

Dancing in silver, the moon
between clouds shining
through

Losing my headphones
is barely anything when
I'm losing sleep

This heavy feeling in my
chest is dark and
deep

Leaving home is nothing
compared to you on a
plane

Wine that I can't drink
going down the
drain

Stay

People come and go
but I wanted you to stay
if love is a hunter
I became the prey

Your toothbrush is
still next to mine
let me gaze in
ocean eyes of thine

Lost I am in frenzied water
as you touch my body
I ache for more and more
from you, not anybody

Birds singing in the morning
as you open your eyes lazy
you are eternal
my heart is beating crazy

We share a blanket
as we share our souls
what future holds we don't
know, there is no goal

Don't go now or
take me with you
I can't stand the pain
of your lack of blue

Forget

I would do anything
to forget I miss you

Would take all pills
to forget the blue

Get high on green
to not see your face

When late at night in
my room I pace

Drink until I'm blacked
out and on the floor

When I think it's enough
that's when I need more

Would do anything
to have you near

But you're far and I'm
alone with my fear

To drown in your ocean
the death I desire

Lost in placid water
choking on the wire

I would do anything
but missing you is crazy

I'm going insane
everything is hazy

Pretty Boy

That's what you called me
before each kiss
I still remember the
warmth of the bliss

Burning my chest
hard to breathe
when it's you and I
in the narrow streets

To be with you
I need more
distant lands and
the seashore

Late at night with closed
eyes I think of how
you held me soft
but you're gone now

I think back and
memories seem fake
I'm living a nightmare
I'm about to break

Call me once again
say pretty boy to me
let our lips meet
fill my lungs with glee

Once more I crave a hug
never let me go
swallow me whole
One thing for sure I know

I see your face at dawn
hear your voice on 9
but if they ask I say
everything is fine

If

If you ever wanna
fall in love
I'll be at reach
my precious dove

If the bed is
too big for you
let me show the
beauty of new

If you are cold
and shaking in night
look at the stars they
shine so bright

If life's too much
you break under pressure
I want to show you
endless treasure

If music stops
playing in your heart
I'll swim through oceans
that tear us apart

If you turn cold
I'll hold you tight
and let you know
it will be all right

If you want to escape
acrid pain
let me be the
drowsy rain

If you are ready
to let go of me
for the last time
let me kiss thee

Please stay with
me and never leave
don't make me again
sink in this grief

Selfish it is
to want you now
when you mourned and
live with it somehow

My lack of presence
still makes your heart ache?
I know that without you
I'll break

Yet someday I might
see your face
don't forget to
keep your grace

9800

You became a number
9800
in my deepest slumber
that's all I've wanted

For you to come back
knowing it is selfish
I could fit in a backpack
all of our memories

My heart is aching
feeling every mile
false blue skies fading
I want to see you smile

But that's the thing
I want you to be glad
do whatever would bring
all the joy I had

My heart sank a bit
when I saw your name
I don't want to
play this game
This black sorrow
pounding my chest
I'm tired, give my
heart some rest
Tell me once more
about your dreams
let me hold you
suffocate your fears
Share a cigarette
to you I'm turning
just like tobacco
my heart is burning
You are still
next to me in bed
I have place for
the memories we had
Cold December
cold is my heart
there are oceans
to tear us apart

I want my hand
held on a train
I want to dance and
kiss in the rain

I want to smile with
someone at night
I want to be told
I will be all right

I want stolen shirts
that are too big
I want to stay up
and share a cig

I want to walk
and gaze at stars
I want to tangle
all of our parts

I search for your
face in every crowd
trying to keep it
together and proud

His smile makes my
heart turn cold
from all the words you
haven't told

Trying to find
the beauty in living
I'm empty but still
giving and giving

Faking laughs and
sharing joy
when deep down
I'm a broken boy

Drowsy mind from
too much wine
drunk on you
but I am fine

Standing strong
yet I still need
your touch or
to death I bleed

And now I go
home to stare
at walls and hope
you still care

Far from me
across the globe
still haven't worn
your purple robe

You're all the colours
in dull world
my silent cries
only you've heard

Balcony

Crying in the moonlight
because you are not
with me tonight

I pray for the night
to not be harsh
so I make it right

When I want to burn
my skin, you are
a wonderful sin

I'll wait for a year
maybe thousands
dry up my tears

Fallen leaf I am
twirling in wind
that's the most I can

Look at me now
and with grace
I will bow

Tonight's endless
I am stupid
and reckless

Will not sleep
breaths I take
are so deep

Wounds are hurting
heart is bleeding
my skin is burning

Soft pain on wrist
my every word
you twist

In your voice it's pity
yet eyes so
blue and pretty

Hurt me once more
make it ache, so I
collapse on the floor

This pain is all
consumes me
still I stand tall

Today's a lonely one
with this grief
I am done

Make me float and sink
I raise my glass with
this last drink

Til' I'm out of mind
it pains me that
you were so kind

Blurry are the skies
in his wallows he
still tries

Inhales cold air
I am here and
you are there

Tired is my soul
this feeling is
grim and foul

I refuse to be ghost
of your dreams
like empty shell tossed

Nightmare it is
to see your smile and
feel this kiss

My pride I swallow
dignity none
this path I follow

Alone or with you
doesn't matter just
make it through

Drowning in wine
ocean eyes of thine

Soft air you are
from me so far

Fine touch it is
still feel the kiss

Lighters you used
the love you refused

Flowers don't bloom
in this winter doom

Embrace of the sun
to me there is none

Windows with light
you are so bright

Smile for me dear
I want you near

Said it before
endless seashore

I'm still trying
keep on smiling
when deep down
there's a hole

Smoke through nights
endless fights
with myself if I
should wait more

Camomile fills
or overused pills
that I got out
from the trash

Vessels with blood
my shoes with mud
because I refuse
all that's new

Reunion

Flutters my heart
such a beautiful part
of me might return
Let me hold you
and maybe you too
will fall in love again
Truly this time
there is no rhyme
let's sink in this glee
Hug me like you feel
how our broken hearts heal
and we might stop time
Endless embrace
let the disgrace
go and fade away
I dream of a kiss
from the one I miss
in this silent night
More than post it notes
or any anecdotes
you were a ray of the sun
Smile is summer breeze
after this month of freeze
my body will defrost
You are bird in sky

there is no why
to my love
When clouds come
all that's undone
will wash away in rain
Keep my voice
and this rejoice
locked up in you
Celebrate the sun
the beauty, the new

When I wear green
My mind echoes "keen"
'cuz that's what
you gave me

When the sky's blue
you have no clue
how bad it pains
my heart

Haven't washed your towel
I ran out of power
it's already been
two months

Days go crazy slow
stars in the night glow
and remind me of
your beamy eyes

The t-shirt I gave you
helps me get through
nights like this when
I fall and crash

My pillow misses
your soft kisses
and the moans
from pleasure

I don't need heaven
there's poems, maybe seven
that are not about
what we had

They were special I swear
all the moments where
we felt like the
world stopped spinning

How could I love you
when I hate who I am
let go of my hand
do it while you can

I'm burning inside
from all that's unsaid
like flowers in summer
my heart is turning red

Still I give a go
smile and yet break
all I see is dark
when the stars fade

Collapse on the ground
it hurts and my lungs
break free from chest
let me taste your tongue

L

There's no rhyme to describe
your heavenly touch
the cheerful cordial vibe
an embrace couldn't be this much

Yet here I am darling
melting in those arms of yours
like my heart is sparkling
I won't admit my love of course

Would be foolish to say
how bad I crave thine soul
but only if I may
want to ask the rain to pour

Meadow in thine eyes
rose garden your cheeks
easing late night cries
conquering highest peaks

With you by my side
impossible is fake
open those arms wide
now it's love we make

Resting souls unite
in this night of silence
no need for us to fight
or engage in violence

Hearts pounding madly
to touch so fierce and aching
release your breath gladly
love is what we're making

The very moment I saw
sparkling eyes of your
my heart filled with pleasure
silent pleasure, of course

Soft motions we made
for the other not to scare
but oh, I ached thine touch
it was hell to try to bare

See you in the morning ray
a little more I wish to stay
in thine arms the world is steady
and my breathing's not so heavy

Trembling souls is what we are
going deep yet not so far
with brave minds we both well know
alone these roads we cannot go

I miss your hand in mine
meadow eyes of thine
uneven breaths slowly rising
a voice so calm and paralyzing

Skin so fierce against each other
with my words I cannot bother
you know my heart, you know it deep
my secret I ask, you to keep

Without you it aches so much
hell of a wait to feel your touch
but as we meet I'm lost in you
tell me that you feel this too

Long time no seen your face
in slumbers heart beating crazy pace
holding your hand like never before
swallowing us, deserted shore

Aching to touch bodies so fierce
sky from ground, apart it tears
I wake up, from bed I crawl
truly I was with you whole

Daytime spent without who I crave
thunderstorms and darkness came
in my sleep our souls unite
it's you and me and just tonight

Hold me now, there's a thunder outside
I await for the sun to shine bright
next to you I am small
I am barely here at all

Let me forget the rain
being late for the train
make me forget the one I miss
I think of him as I steal a kiss

Your green is almost his blue
he is there and I'm close to you
his curls unmatched
with grey hair patched

My lips are shaking
heart is breaking
the world's too big
I'll light a cig

The sun kisses your face
wish I was in her place
so I could hold you close
and remember those

Moments I thought were forever
you are sweet kind and clever
horn melody echoes near
by your side there's nothing I fear

Snippets

Of Thee

Doomed – that's what we are my own one
sinking into clouds, thou my sole saviour
catch the smithereens as I am gone
with stifled heart-sick behaviour

Gaze upon heavenly wreath encompassing
consume my fondness, absorb my words
lost in the mist of time I'm wandering
can I say living – how very much it hurts?

My enchanting – lonesome daffodil who weapt
shed no tear when I am gone
smother all fearsome secrets you kept
you were – are – will be my only one

Memento Mori

Horatius friend, you old prideful sage
taught us many a time, no answer is rage
celebrate the mind, capacity of brain
not just pretty flowers, numb and drowsy rain
Victory is knowledge, we are born to gain
through killing heartaches and neverending pain
the sun is shining just for you
rays applaud for all that's new
vanish into darkness, never give up trying
live life at its best and remember you are dying

Farewell

Farewell to the shimmering sky
which under man, can never be lonely
breathing in the stars I died
each time, you never said sorry
Parting with the grass below
that held my body many a time
you tuneless rustling hero
never knew a single crime
I'm calling you, friend,
meadows enamelled with flowers
in oblivious host we lied
blood in my vein, were you endless power
soft comfort when I cried
Rivers, you frenzied knot around the Earth
silent whispers in my skull
My home you were ever since birth
and yet stifled ripples are dull
Sky is turning grey
grass started to dry
for me meadows pray
drop in the ocean – I powerless to try
Thus, farewell to this place
I – whereas have my grace

I smoke because I'm lonely
I smoke because I'm sad
my lungs are turning black
I smoke to catch my breath

Inhale to numb the pain
exhale to let it go
I smoke to get the feeling
I'm defeating my foe

Battling myself
fume became my words
put an end to it
existence sure hurts

Discourse with the dawn
I tell her why I'm crying
soft embrace I receive
because I feel like dying

Scratching my throat
makes me feel so lively
shaking hands don't matter
this, my story briefly

To pass time I smoke
self-destruction's calming
to light a cigarette
easier than talking

In silence next to me
stand and follow the movement
make it stop or at least
facilitate the tornment

Junkie

Longing, aching for that
flow you feel
rough is the path for
you to heal
Smashing my skull
I crave it bad
the night is dull
it was all I had
Just once more I
swore to me
pill bottles to hide
won't let me be
Place it under tongue
to feel it kicking in
I am still so young
the borderline is thin
Bursting into tears
you control my life
All the demons all my fears
to my throat the knife
Breaking the chain
coffee without pills
endless throbbing pain
crazy morning chills
Locked up in secrets

lies upon lies
washing down the regrets
blurry skies
Be strong, they say
but don't know how
there's no other way
for my soul tonight
Prisoner of mind
addict of the bliss
you are one of a kind
how damn much I miss
Get me high
make me float
reach for the stars
in this ragged boat

Heart, madly pounding in my chest
I am unlit cigarettes
body turns to ash and dust
waking up was all a must
not a thing that I intended
cascet of clay that I rented
A being so young, mortified
my existence falsified
Eager glance at wounded shell
everything is more than well

To Ed

Waiting for the day to pass
gentle moon with silver dress
wash away my sins while I
close my eyes, pretend to die
Aching lung from smoke I breathe
seeing stars became my creed
Liar, that's what people say
late at night for death I pray
Mortal ghost what I've become
all I wish is to be gone
prisoner of flesh and bone
building up my peaky throne
Swollen veins and baggy eyes
On the floor he screams and cries
knuckles bleeding, pang in throat
drown ourselves if life's a boat
I became my own worst nightmare

Been shattered since birth
when got released from dirt
still I try to piece the parts
and live fully the vibrant arts
Walking in the woods at dawn
never better what I had drawn
whisper to me sweet sunflower
lock me in your burning tower

Above an empty shot glass
watched another day pass
summer marks burning my skin
loving you is my greatest sin

Paralized lung, the killer mint
why don't you just take the hint?
I ache for only you tonight
look at the stars, they shine so bright

Respiration picks up the pace
I am hoping life's no race
if it were then I would lose
there's no one else that I would choose

Misery fills the room
I'm not alive, this is my doom
I cannot take this acrid pain
please don't ever stop the rain

I'm fading away
bit by bit
like this cigarette
my heart is lit

Burning in flames
scorching hot
in this bed I
decay and rot

The weight I shed
says how I hurt
shamelessly with
death I flirt

Starving to be
empty and strong
to no one and place
I belong

Oh to be held
someday by you
you saw my colours
the me, that's true